BR

Robyn Gee and Mary Anne Evans

Illustrated by Joseph McEwan

Designed by Graham Round
Edited by Jenny Tyler

Contents

3	Map of Britain	28	On the Road
4	Facts about Britain	30	Going to a Village
5	How to Use this Book	33	Pub Signs
6	Prehistoric Britain	34	Houses
8	Roman Britain	36	In the Countryside
12	Castles	40	At the Seaside
15	Great Houses	42	Fun Things to Do
18	Churches	48	Sports
24	Towns	49	Food
27	In the Shopping Centre	50	London
		58	Useful Addresses and Information
		62	Index

Map key

1. Avon
2. Bedfordshire
3. Berkshire
4. Borders
5. Buckinghamshire
6. Cambridgeshire
7. Central
8. Cheshire
9. Cleveland
10. Clwyd
11. Cornwall
12. Cumbria
13. Derbyshire
14. Devon
15. Dorset
16. Dumfries and Galloway
17. Durham
18. Dyfed
19. East Sussex
20. Essex
21. Fife
22. Gloucester
23. Grampian
24. Greater Manchester
25. Greater London
26. Gwent
27. Gwynedd
28. Hampshire
29. Hereford and Worcester
30. Hertfordshire
31. Highland
32. Humberside
33. Isle of Wight
34. Kent
35. Lancashire
36. Leicestershire
37. Lincolnshire
38. Lothian
39. Merseyside
40. Mid Glamorgan
41. Norfolk
42. Northamptonshire
43. Northumberland
44. North Yorkshire
45. Nottinghamshire
46. Oxfordshire
47. Powys
48. Salop
49. Somerset
50. South Glamorgan
51. South Yorkshire
52. Staffordshire
53. Strathclyde
54. Suffolk
55. Surrey
56. Tayside
57. Tyne and Wear
58. Warwickshire
59. West Glamorgan
60. West Midlands
61. West Sussex
62. West Yorkshire
63. Western Isles
64. Wiltshire

First published in 1979 by Usborne Publishing Ltd, 20 Garrick Street, London WC2E 9BJ, England.

Copyright © 1979 Usborne Publishing Ltd.

The name Usborne and the device are Trade Marks of Usborne Publishing Ltd.

Printed in Belgium.

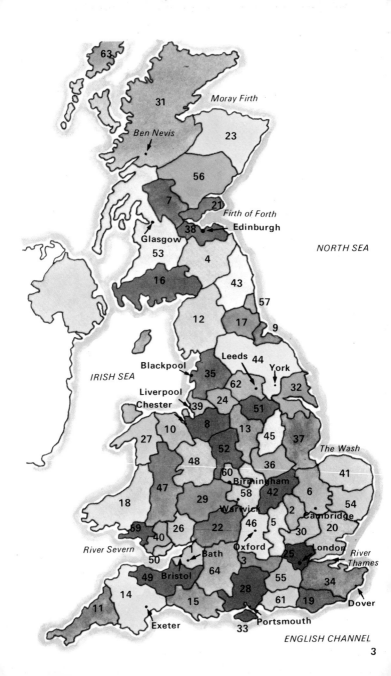

63

31

Moray Firth

23

Ben Nevis

56

7

21

Firth of Forth

38

Edinburgh

Glasgow

NORTH SEA

53

4

16

43

57

12

17

9

IRISH SEA

Blackpool

Leeds

44

York

35

62

32

Liverpool
Chester

39

24

51

8

13

45

37

10

The Wash

27

52

36

48

60

41

47

29

Birmingham

58

42

6

54

18

Warwick

2

Cambridge

26

22

46

5

30

20

59

40

Oxford

25

London

River Severn

50

Bath

3

River
Thames

49

Bristol

64

55

34

14

28

61

19

Dover

11

15

33

Portsmouth

Exeter

ENGLISH CHANNEL

3

Facts About Britain

Great Britain is the biggest of a group of islands called the British Isles, which lies off the north-west coast of Europe. It is divided into three parts: England, Scotland and Wales. Great Britain plus the northern part of Ireland, the second largest of the British Isles, is called the United Kingdom.

Facts and figures

Population: 55,780,000.

5 largest cities: London, Manchester, Birmingham, Glasgow, Leeds.

Highest mountain: Ben Nevis (1392m)

Longest river: Severn (355km).

The Government

Britain is governed by a parliament of 635 elected members. The head of the government is the Prime Minister, who is the leader of the political party with the most members of parliament.

The Queen

Elizabeth II became Queen of the United Kingdom in 1952 and was crowned in 1953. Her oldest son, Prince Charles, is the heir to the throne and if he becomes king he will be King Charles III.

The flag

The Union Jack (the flag of the United Kingdom) was first used in 1801. It combines the red cross of St George of England, the white cross of St Andrew of Scotland and the red cross of St Patrick of Ireland.

Capital cities

The capital city of Britain is London. It has over 7 million people and is the 17th largest city in the world. Edinburgh is the capital of Scotland and Cardiff is the capital of Wales.

Time

During the winter Britain uses Greenwich Mean Time. The clocks are turned forward one hour in March to give British Summer Time. In October they are turned back one hour again.

Language

English is spoken in most of Britain but Welsh is widely used in Wales where school children are taught in Welsh. A few people in Scotland still speak Gaelic.

Money

Britain's currency is pounds sterling. One pound (£1) is equal to 100 pence (p). There are 1 and 2 p coins (bronze), 5, 10, 20 and 50 p coins (silver-coloured) and £1 coins (gold-coloured). The smaller notes are £5, £10 and £20. Scottish notes look different but can be used in Britain. Banks are open between 9.30 am and 3.30 pm on weekdays.

Public holidays

New Year's Day (1 January); Good Friday (date changes each year); Easter Monday* (date changes each year); Christmas Day (25 December); Boxing Day* (26 December). Bank holidays: 2 January**; first Monday in May; last Monday in May; first Monday in August**; last Monday in August*.

*Not in Scotland **Only in Scotland*

How to Use this Book

This book is a guide to some exciting things to see and do in Britain. It tells you about famous sights and unusual but interesting places and suggests some fun things to do. There are lots of interesting things to spot. Some of them are common, others are quite rare or are found only in certain areas of the country. Many of them give you clues about the people who lived in Britain in the past.

Take this book with you when you go on holiday or on a day trip, or read it at home to find out about different parts of the country.

To find out more about the places shown in this book, look at the list of books, addresses and telephone numbers given on pages 58 to 61. These will help you to find out opening times, admission fees and exact addresses of places you want to visit. We have given the counties of most places named in the book. To find out if somewhere is near you, look up the county on page 2 and find it on the map on page 3.

The things to spot have boxes next to them. When you spot them, put a tick in the box. The words in heavy type tell you exactly what you should be ticking for.

Making collections to remind you of places you have visited can be fun. You could collect postcards or photographs, bus and train tickets, entrance tickets and wrappers and paper bags with the names of towns on them, or make lists of unusual signs, shops and pub names. Try making a travel scrapbook.

Prehistoric Britain

You can see many prehistoric remains in Britain. Prehistory is the story of man before written records began. It divides into three main periods: the Stone Age (3000 to 1900BC), the Bronze Age (1900 to 700BC) and the Iron Age (700BC to AD43).

Monolith (also called a Menhir). Single standing stone. Probably put up as religious monument.

Trilithon. Two upright stones supporting a third. Usually part of a stone circle.

Stone circles. Prehistoric people built stone circles called "henges". They probably used them for measuring the movements of the sun and stars and for religious ceremonies.

Stonehenge

One of the most famous prehistoric monuments in Europe. Built over 4000 years ago on Salisbury Plain in Wiltshire. The largest stones reach about 7m above ground and 3m below.

Tool marks. Simple stone hammers were used to shape the stones. You can still see the marks they made.

Heelstone

On 21 June, the longest day, the sun rises over the heelstone and shines into the centre of the circle.

Knob

Socket

Where the trilithons have fallen down you can see the **knobs and sockets** which held them together.

In the Orkney Islands there are the remains of a **Stone Age village** called Skara Brae.

You can see the remains of huts and courtyards at Chysauster, an **Iron Age village** in Cornwall.

Brochs. Tall, round towers built as fortresses in Iron Age. Found in Scotland.

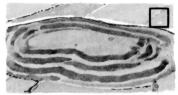

Hill figures have been cut into chalk hillsides in some places. They may have been gods or emblems of tribes. Not all of them are prehistoric.

Hill fort. Hill fortified by ditches and earth banks. Built in the Iron Age, mainly in south of England. This is Maiden Castle in Dorset.

Mounds and tombs

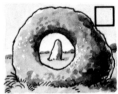

If you see a grassy mound like this one it may be a Stone Age tomb called a **long barrow.**

Inside long barrows are passages and chambers where people were buried.

Stone rings, like this, may have been entrances to burial mounds. They are quite rare.

A round grassy mound might be a Bronze Age tomb called a **round barrow.**

A barrow where the earth has worn away, leaving bare stones, is called a **dolmen.**

Silbury Hill in Wiltshire is a **man-made hill** built by prehistoric people. We do not know why they made it.

Reconstructed farm

At Butser in Hampshire a research team has built an Iron Age settlement and is using Iron Age methods to farm the land.

Looking for flints

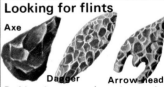

Axe

Dagger   Arrow-head

Prehistoric men made tools out of a hard stone called flint. Look for flint chips and tools if you are near prehistoric remains. They look like this.

Roman Britain 1

The Romans first invaded Britain in AD43. By AD84 they had completed their conquest, although they never really controlled Scotland or the furthest parts of Wales. They ruled for about 350 years and you can still see the remains of many things that they built. This section shows you what to look out for. The map marks the main Roman towns, roads, villas and fortifications.

Villas

Roman villas were large country houses. There are several places in England where you can visit the remains of one. This is a model of the villa at Fishbourne as it probably looked in Roman times.

Mosaic. Pattern made of small pieces of coloured glass, stone or marble. Often used to decorate floors.

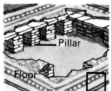

Hypocaust. Part of Roman central heating system. Space under floor heated by hot air from furnace.

Shrine. Many houses had underground shrines or temples where people prayed to their gods.

8

Towns

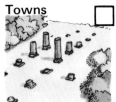  

In a few places the remains of a Roman **forum** (market place) have been uncovered.

You can often spot a **Roman wall** by the line of red tiles running through it.

In some old towns you can see **Roman arches** and bits of their walls.

This is part of the **Roman Baths** at Bath in Avon, which were built above hot springs. They were rebuilt and used long after Roman times.

Look out for archaeologists at work excavating ancient sites. If they dig deep enough they sometimes find Roman remains.

Theatres

You can still see one or two Roman **amphitheatres** (circular arenas surrounded by seats), like this one at Caerleon in Wales. Here people watched shows, chariot races and gladiator fights. They also built semicircular **theatres**. The foundations of the theatre at St Albans are shown above.

Roads

Foundation Stones of Roman road. Roman cities were linked by long straight roads.

Very straight modern roads (not motorways) are often based on the foundations of **Roman roads.**

Milestones marked every Roman mile (1,000 paces) along the roads.

Roman Britain 2

Hadrian's Wall

The Emperor Hadrian built a wall, 122km long, to protect Roman Britain against the warlike tribes who lived in Scotland. You can still see where the wall went.

There was a **milecastle** every 1½km along the wall, each defended by 50 soldiers.

There were 16 **forts** built at intervals along Hadrian's Wall and seven on the south side to give it extra strength. These are the reconstructed defences of the fort at Chesterholm.

Granary at Housesteads. Pillars raised the floor so that air could circulate and keep the corn dry.

Temple at Carrawburgh. Remains of temple where the Roman god Mithras was worshipped before the Romans became Christians.

Dover lighthouse

This is the only Roman lighthouse in Britain still standing. It was originally over 26½m high and fires were kept burning inside it all night. It is one of two which were built at Dover. The other one has now gone.

The Lunt Roman Fort

This is a reconstructed Roman fort near Coventry. Mock battles are staged here by a society called the Ermine Street Guard.

Saxon shore forts

Part of the shore fort at Richborough one of several built to defend the south and east coast against Saxon raiders.

Things to look for in museums

This page shows some things you might see in Prehistoric and Roman collections in museums. Many towns and archaeological sites have museums displaying objects found nearby.

Bronze Age clay beaker found in burial mound. These have patterns of lines scratched on them.

Iron Age helmet. Shields and swords from this period have also been found.

Roman wall painting. Specially good ones are on display at the St Albans Roman Museum.

Roman vase showing gladiators fighting. Many show scenes from Roman life.

Roman coins often have pictures of emperors' heads on them.

Roman glass is very delicate. Jugs like these were made by blowing hot glass into moulds.

Scenes from Roman life. This is a reconstruction of a mosaic craftsman's workshop.

Armour and weapons of Roman soldiers. This model is at Grosvenor Museum, Chester.

Sculpture and statues made by the people living in Roman Britain (left) were much rougher and less life-like than the ones brought from Rome (right).

How to find ancient sites

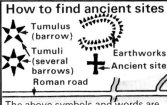

Tumulus (barrow)

Tumuli (several barrows)

Roman road

Earthworks

Ancient site

The above symbols and words are used on Ordnance Survey maps to mark the places where you can find Prehistoric and Roman remains.

Castles

Most English castles were built between 1050 and 1600, when kings and lords needed somewhere to defend their families against enemies. Many were altered and added to as designs changed.

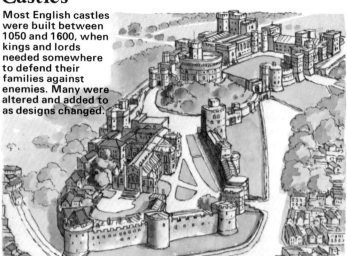

Windsor Castle is one of the homes of the Queen and royal family and is the largest inhabited castle in Europe. It was founded by William the Conqueror, added to over the years and largely rebuilt in the 1820s. You can go inside the Chapel and State Apartments.

Early castles were built on a mound called a **motte** with a court-yard called a **bailey** at the bottom.

Most early stone castles had a **square keep** (main building) like this one at Rochester Castle.

Round keeps, like this, were built because they were easier to defend than square ones.

Later castles were strengthened by outer or curtain walls. These are called **concentric castles.** Edward I built eight of them in Wales.

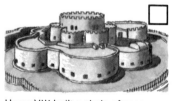

Henry VIII built a chain of **rose-shaped castles** along the coast to protect England from invasion. This is Deal Castle.

Most castles were built of stone but in the last years of castle building a few **brick castles** were built.

In the 1800s it was fashionable to build houses that looked like castles. These are called **Gothic castles**.

Many **Scottish castles** are really fortified houses with the main living rooms on the upper floors.

Jousting

Sham castles, like Mow Cop castle in Cheshire were built to provide romantic views rather than to be lived in.

In the summer, at some castles, people dress up as knights and have mock battles. To find out where jousts are being held, contact the Jousting Association, Chilham Castle, Kent.

Armour and weapons

Look out for these on display at castles.

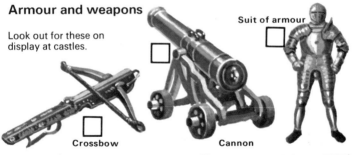

Suit of armour

Crossbow

Cannon

Dungeons

In some castles you can visit the **dungeons.** These are usually underground and very dark and damp.

Torture instruments, like these, were used to punish prisoners or make them talk.

Sometimes you can see the **names and dates** of prisoners scratched on the walls of dungeons.

Things to Spot at Castles

Here are some things to try and spot if you visit a castle. Most of them are things that were useful for keeping out enemies, whose main weapons were bows and arrows, catapults, battering rams and siege towers.

Moat. Deep water-filled ditch surrounding a castle to deter enemies. Some have now been drained.

Drawbridge. Bridge for crossing moat that could be raised or lowered from inside the castle.

Portcullis. Strong wooden and iron grating for blocking gateway. Set in grooves so it can slide up and down.

Arrow slit. Hole in wall through which defenders could fire arrows without becoming targets for their attackers.

Gun-loop. After the invention of cannons, holes through which to fire them were often cut below arrow slits.

Murder holes. Holes in roof of a passage through which things could be dropped on to enemies below.

Machicolations. Holes in parapets or battlements through which stones and weapons were thrown.

Wall-walks between towers gave soldiers a good view of the countryside on all sides when they were on guard.

Spiral staircases, which wind around a central pillar inside towers, connect the separate storeys of a castle.

Fireplace. In ruined castles you often see fireplaces high up on the walls. This shows where floors used to be.

Beam holes. Sometimes in ruined castles you can see the holes where the beams that held up the ceilings fitted.

Great Houses

England is famous for its great country houses. Some are still lived in by the descendants of the noble families who built them, others belong to organizations which keep them in good repair. Most are open to the public at certain times of the year. The houses on this page show how styles of architecture changed over the years. When you visit a great house, see if you can tell which style it belongs to.

Oxburgh Hall, Norfolk, is a fortified manor house built in the 1480s. Early manor houses often have a moat and strong gatehouse like this.

This is Longleat House in Wiltshire, one of the fine country houses built in the Elizabethan age (1558–1603). Many of these are built in the shape of an "E".

In the Jacobean period (1603–1625, when James I was king) brick was a popular building material. This is Hatfield House, Hertfordshire, which was built between 1607 and 1611.

Blenheim Palace, Oxfordshire, (built 1705–1722) is in the Classical style, which was copied from Ancient Greece and Rome. This style has lots of columns.

Harewood House, Yorkshire (built 1759–1771) has a central building with "wings" attached at either end, like most large houses built in the Georgian period (1714–1830).

The Royal Pavilion in Brighton is in a style of its own. The outside looks Indian, the inside Chinese. It was built for the Prince Regent, who later became George IV.

In Victorian times (1837–1901) many houses, like Knebworth House in Hertfordshire, were rebuilt in a style called Gothic, which was first used in the Middle Ages.

Things to Spot in Great Houses

Minstrels' gallery.
Balcony in Great Hall used by musicians who played at feasts.

Painted ceiling.
These often illustrate myths or famous stories.

Secret door. Blends with wall so it is hidden when closed.

Linenfold panelling.
Design in wood panelling which looks like draped cloth.

Fire screen. Used by ladies to shield their faces from the heat of the fire.

Silent companions.
Painted wooden figures, usually by fires, said to keep ladies company.

Four-poster bed. The curtains were drawn at night to give privacy and keep out draughts.

Basin and jug. Before houses had bathrooms, maids brought water for washing to the bedrooms.

Bellrope. When this was pulled a bell rang in the servants' part of the house.

Warming pan. These were filled with hot coals and used for warming and airing beds.

Spit for roasting meat over a fire. A boy turned the handle so meat cooked on all sides.

Mirror with candles.
The light was reflected by the mirror and so made the room brighter.

Family crests

Many families have their own coat-of-arms, something like this, which is passed down through the generations.

Metal stamps for making **wax seals** on documents often have the crest from the coat-of-arms on them. □

Coats-of-arms are often used as decoration, specially over doorways and fireplaces. □

Portraits

See if you can spot any family likenesses between the people in the paintings in the house. They are often ancestors of the family who owns the house.

Ghosts

If you visit an old house ask if it is supposed to be haunted. This is the ghost of Catherine Howard, the fifth wife of Henry VIII, who is said to haunt Hampton Court.

Gardens

□

Knot Garden. Low box hedges divide the flower beds into elaborate patterns.

□

Topiary. Shrubs clipped into ornamental shapes, often of birds or animals.

□

Sundial. A shadow cast by the sun falls on a surface marked with hours and shows you the time.

□

Temple. At one time it was fashionable to build mock temples as garden ornaments.

□

Maze. Complicated network of paths with high hedges on either side. There is only one way to the centre and back again so it is easy to get lost in them.

17

Churches 1

Looking round churches can be fun if you have things to look out for. On the next few pages, you will find some clues to the age of a church, a selection of things to spot in them and some information about different types of churches. Before you go into a church to look round it, make sure there is not a service in progress. There are usually several services on Sundays.

Cathedrals

A **cathedral** is a large church which contains the throne of a bishop or archbishop. There are 56 in Britain, many of which are famous for their architecture.

The **West Front** is often elaborately decorated with stone carvings.

The clergymen who run the cathedral have meetings in the **chapter house**.

See if you can find the **bishop's throne** or *cathedra* (Greek word for seat).

Cathedrals that were once monastery churches have **cloisters**. These are covered arcades round a square where the monks could walk and meditate.

Some churches were once part of a monastery or nunnery and the old name of abbey is still used for a few, like Bath Abbey. Others are now called cathedrals.

Ruined abbeys

There are many ruined abbeys (once monasteries and nunneries) in Britain. Most of them were destroyed by Henry VIII between 1536 and 1540, when he broke away from the Catholic Church.

If you visit a **ruined abbey,** see if you can find the part where the monks slept (the dormitory) and where they ate (the refectory). There is usually a plan of how it used to look on a notice board or in a guide book.

Churches

There are over 19,000 parish churches in Britain. In many towns and villages, the church is the oldest building. For centuries, it was the centre of the community and so it can tell you a lot about local history.

Look out for yew trees in the churchyard. They may be even older than the church. Also look for a weathervane on the steeple. The most common is a cock, the symbol of St Peter.

Chapels

Large churches often have several chapels in them. The **lady chapel** is usually behind the main altar.

Chantry chapels, often with railings round them, were paid for by people who wanted prayers said for them.

Regimental chapels are for the special use of an army regiment. They usually have the regiment's flag in them.

Sometimes chapels were built in remote areas because the main church was too far away. These are called **chapels of ease.**

Some independent religious groups, like the Methodists, call their places of worship **chapels.**

Organs

Organs have been used in churches for hundreds of years, but for a long time only important churches had them. Until the middle of the last century smaller churches used a band of musicians playing recorders, fiddles and cellos.

The organ is usually in a loft or gallery. Look for the long pipes. Each one plays a different note when air is let in.

The organist has keyboards and a panel of stops to work with his hands, and pedals for his feet.

Things to Spot in Churches

Gargoyle. Stone spout to keep water from gutter clear of wall. Usually carved in the shape of an ugly head.

Flying buttresses. Arches on the outside of a building which act as props to hold the walls in place.

Sanctuary door knocker. In the Middle Ages, anyone who touched it could claim sanctuary and be safe from arrest.

Hammer-beam roof. Type of wooden roof that has no cross beams to support it. Often beautifully carved.

Fan vaulting. Stone roof with ribs branching out like the sticks of a fan.

Roof boss. Ornament placed where the ceiling ribs meet. Often carved and painted like this one.

Box pew. Pew with high wooden sides. You get in and out through a door.

Poppy-head bench-end. Decoration on the top of a bench-end. There are many different poppy-head designs.

Misericord. Hinged seat in choir stall for resting on during long services. The underside is often carved.

  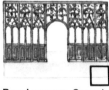

Rose window. Round window usually filled with tracery (patterns made by thin strips of stone).

Squint. Opening in an inside wall which gives a view of the high altar, when it was hidden by a rood screen.

Rood screen. Carved wood or stone screen which separates the altar from the congregation.

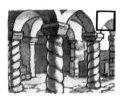

Crypt. Underground room beneath most cathedrals and large churches. People were sometimes buried here.

Eagle lectern. Wood or brass eagle with outstretched wings for holding an open Bible.

Carved font cover. Often so heavy it has to be lifted by chains (The font holds water for Christenings.)

Pulpit with sounding board to reflect the preacher's voice towards the congregation.

Pulpit with hour glass to tell preachers how long they have been talking for. Often, only the iron bracket is left.

Chained Bible. You can sometimes see Bibles that were chained for safe-keeping when books were very valuable.

Tombs

 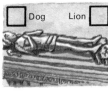 Dog Lion

If the figure on the tomb is a knight with **crossed legs** he was probably a crusader.

If the figure on a tomb rests his **feet on a lion** it means he died at war, if his feet **rest on a dog** he died at home.

The kneeling figures on this tomb are called **weepers.** They represent mourning members of the dead person's family.

Sometimes tombs of very holy people show a **skeleton beneath the main figure** to make people think about death.

From the 1540s onwards figures in casual attitudes became popular. A favourite position was **leaning on one elbow.**

Some early tombs have **niches for receiving pilgrims' offerings** cut into the sides.

Churches 2

Clues to the age of a church

You can tell from the style in which a church is built roughly how old it is, although some churches have been restored and added to in a mixture of styles. Here are the names of the main styles used in the Middle Ages, when most British churches were built.

Norman	1066-1189
Early English	1189-1307
Decorated	Gothic 1307-1327
Perpendicular	1327-1509

To date a church, try matching its doors, windows and overall shape to the pictures below. You will also see Gothic features in Victorian churches (1837-1901). These are often built of brick, so they are fairly easy to spot.

Towers and spires

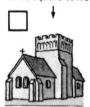 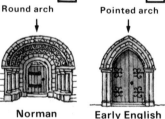  

Low, square tower

Tall spire

Sharply pointed spire

Tall, square tower

Norman   Early English   Decorated   Perpendicular

Doors

Round arch

Pointed arch

Arch less sharply pointed

Square frame above arch

Norman   Early English   Decorated   Perpendicular

Windows

Round arch

Pointed arch

Elaborate stone patterns

Delicate stone patterns

Norman   Early English   Decorated   Perpendicular

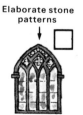
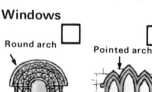
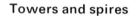

Pictures in churches

In the days when most people could not read and write, painted, carved and glass pictures in churches helped people to learn Bible stories. You will often see **stained glass windows showing Bible scenes.** This one shows Adam and Eve with the serpent in the Garden of Eden.

Wallpaintings have survived in only a few churches. The Last Judgement, showing Jesus judging people's souls at the end of the world, is a common subject.

Brasses

You will often see brass plates, engraved with pictures of people, fixed to the walls and floors of churches. They were put up as memorials to dead people. You can take rubbings from them, but you must ask permission from the vicar first and usually pay a small fee. There are also several brass-rubbing centres where you can rub copies of brasses.

To do a brass-rubbing you need paper, tape and heelball wax. First tape the paper down over the brass, then rub the wax over the paper until the complete image has appeared on the paper.

In some churches, there are **pictures carved round the tops of pillars.** This one from Wells Cathedral shows a farmer hitting a fruit thief over the head.

Church bells

Most churches have a set of bells hung in the tower. Each one plays a different note and bellringers ring them in changing sequences by pulling on long ropes. Look for the **bell ropes** tied up against the wall.

The pictures on **brasses** are usually of important people, like bishops, lords, ladies, knights and merchants. The oldest ones date from the 1200s.

Roman numerals in dates

Dates on old buildings are often given in Roman numbers, like this: MDCCXLIII (1743). Here is how to work them out. I = 1, V = 5, X = 10, L = 50, C = 100, D = 500, M = 1000. Where a number comes before a number larger than itself, subtract e.g. IV = 4 (5 − 1), IX = 9 (10 − 1). Otherwise add the numbers together e.g. VII = 7 (5 + 1 + 1).

Towns 1

Edinburgh, the capital city of Scotland, is built on hills and crags. This is Princes Street, the main shopping street.

York has many streets which were built in the Middle Ages and have changed little since then. This one is in the area called the "Shambles".

Chester also has buildings from the Middle Ages. The "Rows", shown above, are open passages along the first floor of the houses, with shops leading off them.

Warwick grew up around a castle. This 14th century building is Lord Leicester's Hospital, built for poor people to live in.

Bath. Famous for its hot springs since Roman times. Much of it, including the Royal Crescent (above), was built in the 1700s.

Stratford-upon-Avon. William Shakespeare was born here. This is the Royal Shakespeare Theatre where his plays are performed.

Oxford. Famous for its university. The round building is the Sheldonian Theatre, used for university ceremonies and concerts.

Cambridge. Also famous for its university. Here you can see people punting on the river Cam, in front of King's College.

Things to look for

Towns used to be surrounded by **city walls** for protection. In some old towns you can still see them.

City walls had **gateways** in them. These were the only way in and out of the town and were closed at night.

In the Middle Ages many town houses were built with **overhanging storeys.** This made the streets very dark.

Before tarmac and concrete, road surfaces were made of stones. Small irregular stones are called **cobbles.**

Gas lamps, made from ornate iron, were used to light the streets. Many have now been converted to electricity.

An **old-fashioned street name** often tells you what was sold in that street.

A **porte-cochère** (coach door) is an archway to the courtyard of an inn or house, wide enough for a coach and horses.

Old-fashioned shop signs showed symbols of the shopkeepers' trades. **Three gold balls** is the sign for a pawnbroker's shop.

Victorian pillar boxes have VR on them, which stands for *Victoria Regina* (Latin for queen). They are often six-sided.

Many town parks have a **bandstand,** where a band plays in summer. The fashion for these started in the early 1800s.

Local residents sometimes decorate their area with **wall-paintings,** on the sides of buildings.

Walls with stubs of iron on top once had railings. The iron was cut down and used to make weapons in World War II.

Towns 2

Things to spot on buildings

Mason's mark. When a stonemason worked on a building he often signed it with his mark and the date.

Link snuffer. Used to put out flaming torches, which were carried to light the way before there were street lamps.

Fire insurance sign. Showed which company had insured a building because each one had its own fire brigade.

Twisted chimney stack. Built in Tudor times (1485–1603). They are made of brick and are often patterned.

Blocked up windows. From 1695 to 1851 there was a tax on windows so people blocked them up to avoid paying it.

Wall anchors help to hold outside walls straight. They are attached to beams or rods inside the building.

Local museums

Objects, like these Saxon brooches, give clues about the people who lived in the area a long time ago.

Some museums, like the Castle Museum in York, have made reconstructions of parts of the town as they used to be. You can walk through cobbled streets, lit by gas lamps and go into old shops.

Tools and machinery, like this spinning jenny used for making cotton, tell you about working life in the past.

The houses of famous people are sometimes turned into museums. This is the room where Shakespeare was born.

Some museums produce leaflets which tell you where to go to spot historic things around town.

In the Shopping Centre

One of Britain's most famous shops, Marks and Spencer, began as a stall in Leeds market in 1884. It became known as Marks' Penny Bazaar, as nothing cost more than a penny. There are now 280 Marks and Spencer shops in Britain.

Co-op shops share their profits among their customers by giving them trading stamps.

Off licences are shops with a special licence allowing them to sell alcohol for people to take away.

Building societies lend money to people wanting to buy or build houses. They will also keep your money in a savings account.

Bookmakers, sometimes called turf accountants, are shops where people can make bets on sporting and other events.

Shop signs

Here are some signs and symbols to look out for in shopping centres. The ones on the bottom row you will see at petrol stations.

Finefare
(Supermarket)

W. H. Smith
(Stationers & newsagents)

Mothercare
(Everything for babies & children)

Barclays Bank

Lloyds Bank

National Westminster Bank

Midland Bank

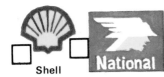

Shell

National

Mobil

British Petroleum

27

On the Road

Finding the way

Most road maps use the following colours:

- ▬▬ — M (motorway)
- ▬ ▬ — Unfinished motorway
- ▬▬ — A (main road)
- ▬▬ — B (secondary road)

Places where you can get on and off motorways are numbered. Check the key on the map you are using.

Road signs

Signs in red triangles warn of dangers ahead. Here are a few. See how many more you can spot.

Quayside or river bank

Wild animals

Slippery road

Falling or fallen rock

Humpback bridge

Boundary signs

Croeso i Cymru
Welcome to Wales

CITY OF CHICHESTER

Look out for interesting boundary signs. They often show coats-of-arms, or emblems, like the red dragon on the boundary sign of Wales.

Tolls

Travellers used to have to stop at **tollhouses** and pay for using the road.

You still have to pay at a **tollbooth** before crossing some bridges.

AA

The AA (Automobile Association) is a motorists' club, which gives its members advice and helps them when their cars break down. This is an **AA patrolman** with his **van**.

RAC

The RAC (Royal Automobile Club) is also a motorists' club, like the AA, and it offers similar services to its members. This is an **RAC patrolman** with his **van**.

Vehicles to spot

Mini. Smallest four-wheeled car made in Britain. First made in 1959.

Range Rover. Comfortable car also suitable for very rough conditions. Introduced in 1970.

Rolls Royce. Luxury car, famous throughout the world for its good quality and high cost.

Car transporter. Takes cars from factories to garages to be sold, or to docks for export.

Concrete-mixing lorry. As it travels it mixes gravel, cement and water to make concrete.

Breakdown truck. Lifts the front of a broken-down car with its winch to make towing easier.

Fire engine. There are different models in use but they are all red with blue flashing lights.

Articulated lorry. Has a pivot between cab and rest of lorry to make turning easier.

Tanker. Lorry with tank for carrying liquids like milk, oil and petrol.

Cars from abroad

Cars registered abroad have letters to show which countries they come from. Here are some letters and the countries they stand for. See how many you can spot.
British cars show the letters GB when they go abroad.

A	— Austria	I	— Italy
AUS	— Australia	IRL	— Ireland
B	— Belgium	L	— Luxembourg
CDN	— Canada	M	— Malta
CH	— Switzerland	N	— Norway
CY	— Cyprus	NL	— Netherlands
D	— Germany	NZ	— New Zealand
DK	— Denmark	P	— Portugal
E	— Spain	S	— Sweden
F	— France	SF	— Finland
FL	— **Liechtenstein**	USA	— United States
GR	— Greece		of America

Going to a Village

Here are some things to look out for when you visit a village. Many villages grew up in the Middle Ages and some of the things you see will date from that time. Look out for dates on old buildings.

Manor House or Hall. Usually the largest house in the village. The Lord of the Manor used to live here.

Pub. Might be several hundred years old. Look out for a date on the sign or carved over the door.

Old school building. Usually about 100 years old. Sometimes has separate entrances for boys and girls.

Almshouses. These were built by rich men as homes for old people. They are often long low buildings or rows of cottages, and have tall chimneys.

Earliest date

The churchyard is often the oldest part of the village. Look at the names and dates on the tombstones. See which is the **earliest date** you can find. You might find several graves with the same family name on them.

A churchyard gate with a roof is called a **lych-gate.** "Lych" is the old English word for dead body.

Crosses

Celtic cross. Often not cross-shaped, but has cross carved on. Very old. Put up by early Christians.

Market cross. Might be called a Butter Cross or Wool Cross, according to what was usually sold there.

War memorial. This is a reminder of people who died in war. See which war it commemorates.

Punishments in the Middle Ages

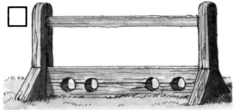

Stocks. People had to sit with their feet locked through the holes.

Whipping post. People were tied to this post and then whipped.

Ducking stool. Women who nagged were put on one of these and ducked in the pond.

Pillory. The lawbreaker stood on the platform and his head and hands went through the holes.

Lock-up. A small, solid building with no windows which was used as an overnight prison.

Other village things

Pound. Stray animals were caught and put in here. Their owners had to pay to get them back.

Dovecote. People used to eat doves (pigeons). They kept the birds in stone huts like this.

Tethering post. This was where people tied up their horses.

Horse trough. Stone basin filled by rain for animals to drink from.

Pump. Water was often drawn up from underground by pump before villages had mains water supply.

Well. A bucket on a rope reaching down to the underground water. To raise it, you wind the handle.

Different Types of Village

Villages grew up in different places for different reasons. You can often tell from its shape why a particular village started where it did. Here are some examples. See if you can spot villages like these.

Some villages are grouped round a **village green,** which is common land belonging to the whole village. There is sometimes a duck pond in the middle. Finchingfield in Essex is a good example of this type of village.

Often a village lies in the **bend of a river.** Originally the river would have supplied water and been a good defence against raiders.

Some villages grew up **along a busy highway,** often a trade route. These are long and narrow. Broadway in Worcestershire is like this.

Many villages are grouped **around a crossroads** because, in the old days, this was a good place to trade.

Villages on the coast are usually grouped **around a harbour or bay** instead of a green. This is Mevagissey, a fishing village on the coast of Cornwall.

Sometimes villages grew up **around a castle or monastery.** At Dunster, in Somerset, the castle is at the top of the hill and the village is at the bottom.

In mountainous areas, like Wales, villages grew up **on the side of the valleys.** Many Welsh villages look like this.

Pub Signs

As you travel about, it is fun to spot pub signs. There are thousands of different names for pubs, but here are some of the main types. When you spot a sign, see if you can tell which of these types it is.

A bush was the original trade sign for a drinking house. "The Grapes" and "The Chequers" are also early pub names.

Some pubs started as inns that provided food, drink and lodging for pilgrims, merchants and other travellers.

Some pub names have a religious meaning. "The Star" gets its name from the Star of Bethlehem.

Many pubs used the name of the local lord and painted his coat-of-arms and family motto on the sign.

There are lots of pubs named in honour of the kings and queens of England.

Sometimes pubs take their names from famous events. This one is called after Nelson's great victory at sea.

Some pubs are called after famous people. Dick Turpin was a well-known highwayman.

In country districts, you often see signs connected with farming or local trades and crafts.

You will probably see lots of pubs with the names of birds, animals and fishes.

Look out for pubs with names taken from a sport. These are not very common.

There are lots of pubs with joke signs. Here the "load of mischief" is the man's wife.

Houses

Here are some old houses to spot. In the past, people usually built houses out of local materials and many areas developed their own particular style of building.

Rough stone walls and slate roof. You will see a lot of cottages like this in Scotland, Wales, Ireland and Cornwall.

Cob and thatch. Walls made of a mixture of clay, gravel and straw, called cob. Roof of straw or reeds.

Cruck-framed. Crucks are curved wooden beams which reach from the ground to the roof and support the house.

Box-framed. These houses are made of a wooden frame, painted black, which is filled in with plaster, usually painted white.

Limestone. This golden coloured stone is found mainly in the area called the Cotswolds. The stones are usually smooth and neat.

Flint. This is a very hard, steely grey stone, found in chalky areas. Flint houses often have brick frames round the doors and windows.

Tile-hung. Tiles are hung over wood and plaster houses to protect them from bad weather. You will see lots of these in Kent.

Weather-boarded. Wooden boards are fixed across the walls to protect them from the weather. You will sometimes see half-weather-boarded houses.

Roofs

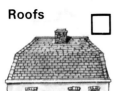

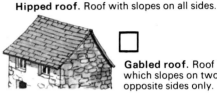

Hipped roof. Roof with slopes on all sides.

Mansard roof. Roof with two slopes on each side, the lower one steeper than the upper.

Gabled roof. Roof which slopes on two opposite sides only.

"M"-shaped gable. Two gabled roofs side-by-side.

Crow-steps or corbie-steps. Step shapes at the end of gabled roof.

Dutch gable. Curly shape at the edge of a roof.

Thatch

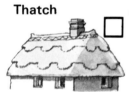

You can see **thatched roofs** in most parts of Britain. They are usually made from straw, reeds or heather.

Look out for **bird and animal shapes** on the top of thatched buildings. They are often thatchers' trademarks.

Sometimes **church roofs** are thatched, though this is quite rare.

Notice board

Wall

Bus stop

35

In the Countryside 1

Here are some things to spot as you travel through the countryside. They are all things that you can see from the roads, though some of them are quite unusual, so you will have to keep your eyes open.

Post windmill. Almost the whole building turns on an oak post, so that the sails face the wind.

Cap windmill. Has a roof, or cap, which turns round so that the sails face the wind.

Watermill. Built beside a river or stream which turns the water-wheel.

Water tower. Stores water high above the ground so that when needed it flows well.

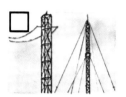

Radio and television masts transmit signals from broadcasting stations. Red lights on top warn planes.

Canals and rivers

Painted narrow boat. These were built to carry goods along canals. The boatmen and their families lived on them and decorated them with brightly-coloured patterns.

Locks. Help boats to change level, where canals go up or down hill. The water level between two gates is gradually raised or lowered.

Tow-path. Path used by horses or gangs of men who towed boats along the canals.

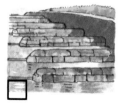

Salmon ladder. Steps built in river to help salmon go upstream to their breeding grounds.

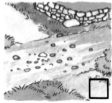

Ford. Shallow place in a river crossed by a road.

36

Bridges

Clapper bridge. Very old type of bridge made of huge granite slabs resting on rock piles.

Hump-backed bridge. Steeply-arched stone bridge.

Bridge with "V"-shaped alcoves where people can stand to avoid traffic.

Iron bridge. The first ones were built in the early 1800s.

Suspension bridge. A roadway hung on huge cables from turrets at either end.

Cow bridge. Bridge for animals to cross, in places where a main road divides a farmer's land.

Viaduct. Arches which carry a road or railway line across a valley. This is Ribble Head Viaduct in Yorkshire.

Aqueduct. Man-made channel built to carry water. This is the Pont-Cysyllte Aqueduct in Wales. It is 305m long and has 19 arches.

The National Trust

An organization which looks after places of historic interest and natural beauty. It owns about 200 square kilometres of land, most of which is open to the public.

National Parks

Ten specially wild and beautiful areas in England and Wales which are protected by law from any development which might spoil the landscape. Each one has a different sign.

The Forestry Commission

An organization which plants and looks after trees, especially quick-growing conifers. In its Forest Parks it provides picnic and camping sites and lays out nature trails.

In the Countryside 2

Farms

Most of the British countryside is owned by farmers. Here are some things to spot on farms. Types of farms vary according to the soil and climate of the area, so some of these things can be seen only in certain places.

Dutch barn. Open-sided barn used for storing hay and straw.

Old granary. Built on mushroom-shaped "staddle" stones to keep out damp and rats.

Silo. Airtight building in which green crops are pressed to make winter food for animals.

Oast house. Used for drying hops, which help to flavour beer. Many are now used as homes.

Scarecrow. Stick dressed in old clothes to scare birds away from growing crops.

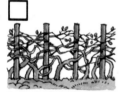

Laid hedge. The young shoots in a hedge are woven round stakes to make it grow thick.

Dry stone wall. Has no cement between the stones. Needs great skill to build. Common in hilly areas.

Stiles. Steps over walls, fences or hedges. Here are four different kinds.

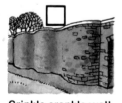

Crinkle crankle wall. Wiggles in and out. Found mainly in Suffolk, often round orchards.

Kissing gate. Old name for a gate swinging in a forked piece of fence. Animals cannot get through.

Cattle grid. Stops sheep and cows crossing but drivers do not have to open and close gates.

Farm machines

A plough, pulled by a tractor, digs up the land into furrows ready for a new crop to be planted.

A seed drill, pulled by a tractor, cuts grooves in the soil and drops seeds into them.

A combine harvester cuts the corn and separates the grain from the stalks.

A baler gathers up the straw (stalks), presses it into bales and ties them with string or wire.

Most **hay and straw bales** are rectangular but sometimes you will see big round ones.

Crops

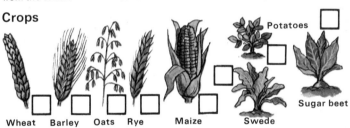

Wheat Barley Oats Rye Maize Swede Potatoes Sugar beet

Here are some of the most common types of crop grown in Britain.
See if you can spot them growing.

Hops are climbing plants. You will see tall poles and strings for them to grow up, in hop fields.

Mustard and a plant called **rape** have bright yellow flowers. They are usually grown for cattle food.

If you are in the flat parts of eastern England called the Fens in spring, look out for fields full of **tulips and daffodils.**

At the Seaside

Seaside holidays first became popular in the 18th century. In the 19th century, railways made it much easier to get to seaside resorts. You can still see some of the entertainments that were popular then.

Piers were first built as landing stages for ships, but by the 1860s they had become popular as pleasure promenades with amusements on them.

Donkey rides on the sands date from the late 1700s. They were probably started by gypsies.

Seaside rock with letters in it was first made in the 1860s. Traditionally, it is pink and white.

Punch and Judy puppet shows began in Italy and came to England in the 1660s.

Mooring buoy

Tide mark

Lobster pot

Bollard, for tying boats up to

Here are some things to spot in small harbours used by fishing and pleasure boats.

Martello tower. Round forts built in the early 1800s when people thought Napoleon might try to invade England.

Pill-box. Concrete look-out posts built to guard the coasts during World War II.

Shapes and patterns in the cliffs

Cliffs at the seaside are good places for looking at rocks because they are not covered in earth, so you can see the different layers of which they are formed.

Movements under the earth cause rocks to split and shift. A break in layers of rock is called a **fault**.

Places where layers of rock have been buckled by movements under the earth's surface are called **folds**.

A pillar of rock, separated from a headland when the rock in between wears away, is called a **stack**.

Where caves form on both sides of a headland, the waves sometimes break through and make an **arch**.

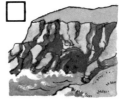

Cracks in the rocks get wider and the waves break against them. Some of the cracks become **caves**.

Guarding the coasts

The best way to find out about life in a **lighthouse** is to visit one. There are about 80 in Britain which you can see round.

You can go inside many of Britain's 200 **lifeboat stations** and see the boat.

Coastguards keep watch for ships in trouble and other emergencies from **coastguard stations**.

Fireworks or sirens call the volunteer crew in an emergency. Look out for a **lifeboat at sea**.

Tides and currents make some parts of the British coast dangerous for swimmers, especially in windy weather. Never swim when red warning flags are flying. The safest time to swim is when the tide is coming in, or at high tide.

Fun Things to Do 1

British Rail stopped using **steam trains** in 1968. But they have now become so popular that railway enthusiasts are allowed to run special excursions on main lines. There are also several private lines. This train is in Oakworth station on the private Keighley and Worth Valley line.

In Wales, there are several **small steam railways.** They run on narrow-gauge tracks and operate mainly in the summer.

There are several **miniature railways** in Britain, but the Romney, Hythe and Dymchurch line in Kent is the world's only mainline miniature railway.

There are several **old ships** you can go aboard. This is H.M.S. Victory, Nelson's flagship at the Battle of Trafalgar, at Portsmouth.

You can go for **boat trips** on most big lakes and rivers. Look out for the monster if you go on Loch Ness.

In **model villages,** everything is on a miniature scale so that you feel like a giant. At Bekonscott in Buckinghamshire the village includes a castle, a zoo and a railway.

At most **airports** there is a viewing platform from which you can watch aeroplanes taking off and landing.

A **camera obscura** is a room used as a camera. Images from outside the room are reflected on to a table.

Cheddar, in Somerset is one of the places where you can see **caves** with stalagmites and stalactites.

In petrifying **wells** objects are coated in stone by lime in the water. You can see one at Knaresborough (Yorks).

The **Dr Who Exhibition** at Longleat has models and monsters used in the filming of the BBC television series.

You can meet Santa Claus and ride on his sleigh at any time of the year in **Santa Claus Land,** at Aviemore in Scotland.

This Viking ship is at **Thorpe Park,** near Staines, which shows the history of Britain as a seafaring nation.

Watching people at work

Many factories and craft centres will let you come and watch people at work, but you often have to make a special appointment, well in advance. Local tourist boards can usually give you a list of such places. Here are some activities that you can usually go and watch without making arrangements in advance.

Several well-known **glass factories,** such as Dartington (Devon) and Caithness (Scotland), give tours which show you every stage in the process of making glass.

You can often visit **potteries** and watch people making pots. Look out for signs as you travel around.

In villages, you can sometimes see **blacksmiths** at work, making horseshoes and iron objects.

Many **windmills** have recently been restored. Here at North Leverton in Nottinghamshire, the mill grinds corn.

Fun Things to Do 2

You may think that museums are boring, but there are lots of really exciting ones. Here are a few. Most of these specialize in a particular subject and in several you can touch the exhibits and even have rides on them.

Transport museums

The **National Railway Museum** in York has the largest collection of railway relics in Britain. Several engines are still in working order.

The **National Motor Museum** at Beaulieu tells the story of motoring from 1895 to modern times. Over 200 vehicles are on display.

There was once a famous ship-building yard at **Buckler's Hard**. Now its Maritime Museum displays models of the ships once built here.

This is one of the many unusual boats on show at **Exeter Maritime Museum**. The larger boats are afloat and you can go aboard and explore them.

At the **Tramway Museum,** Crich, Derbyshire you can take rides on horse-drawn, steam and electric trams, all of which were once used in big cities.

The historic aeroplanes in the **Shuttleworth Collection,** near Biggleswade, are kept in working order.

The **Waterways Museum** at Stoke Bruerne tells you about life on the canals. This is the inside of a narrow boat.

The **London Transport Museum** displays public transport used in London through the ages.

Other interesting museums

Noah's Arks have been popular toys for about 200 years. This is in Edinburgh's **Museum of Childhood**.

The **Llandudno Doll Museum** has over 1,000 dolls. This is a doll, used by tailors to model fashions.

The **Museum of Costume** in Bath shows fashionable dress from the 17th century onwards.

The **Ironbridge Gorge Museum** is an open-air museum which covers the area around the world's first iron bridge. It tells you about industry in the past.

At the **Gladstone Pottery Museum** in Staffordshire, you can see demonstrations of traditional pottery making. The pots used to be fired in these "bottle ovens".

This old market hall is in the **Weald and Downland Open-Air Museum** in Sussex. The museum rescues and rebuilds historic buildings from south-east England.

At the **Beamish North of England Open-Air Museum** you can see cottages and farms as they were 100 years ago. There is also a steam train, an old station and a colliery.

The **Musical Museum** at Brentford in Middlesex has a fascinating collection of automatic pianos, organs and music boxes. All of them are in working order.

The **American Museum** in Bath shows how people in America have lived over the past few hundred years. This is a full-size model of a Red Indian tepee.

Fun Things to Do 3

Zoos and safari parks

By far the largest collection of birds and animals is the British national collection at London Zoo, but there are a large number of smaller collections throughout the rest of Britain. Here are a few suggestions of interesting places to visit.

The Lions of Longleat (opened 1966) was the first drive-through safari park in Europe.
At first it had only lions but now it has a wide variety of birds and animals, mainly from Africa.

Bristol Zoo, the second oldest in Britain, is one of the few in the world which has white tigers.

Whipsnade zoo specializes in herds of animals. It has several rare species, including white rhinos.

Twycross zoo park has the best collection of apes and monkeys in Britain. These are rare proboscis monkeys.

Most zoos have an aquarium, but one of the best is at Chester (the second largest zoo in the country), where you can see sea-horses.

Feeding times for the different animals are usually shown on notice boards. In Edinburgh, the penguins parade through the zoo before they are fed.

Several zoos and safari parks now have dolphinaria where you can see dolphins performing tricks. They jump high out of the water and throw and catch balls.

Most zoos have a pets' corner or childrens zoo. These are special areas where you can get a closer look at the animals, and often you are allowed to stroke them.

Wildlife parks

The Norfolk Wildlife Park and Pheasant Trust has the largest collection of European animals, like this badger, in the world. It also has many rare species of pheasants.

In the Highland Wildlife Park you can see a wide selection of animals that either used to live in the area or, like this wild cat, still do but are not easy to see.

Nature trails

The Slimbridge Wildfowl Refuge has the world's largest display of flamingoes, geese, swans and ducks. This is the brilliantly coloured mandarin duck.

Many parks and forests have nature trails which you can follow. Signs and leaflets tell you about the birds, animals and plants you might see.

Farm parks

If you are interested in farms and farm animals, you might enjoy a visit to a farm park. At Easton Farm Park, Suffolk, you can watch the herd of cows being milked.

Many farm parks and farm museums show you old-fashioned methods of farming. Many things that used to be done by hand are now done by machine.

Special collections

The Otter Trust in Suffolk protects and breeds otters, which are endangered animals.

Worldwide Butterflies in Dorset has the biggest collection of living butterflies in Britain.

The Falconry Centre, Gloucestershire has flying falcon displays and a superb collection of birds of prey.

Sports

The soccer (football) season lasts from August to April. The highlight of the season is the F.A. Cup Final held at Wembley Stadium in London in May.

Amateur, 15-a-side teams play Rugby Union and, in the north of England, professional 13-a-side teams play Rugby League. You can see both every winter Saturday.

In the summer, county cricket teams play in various competitions, like the Nat West Trophy and the Benson and Hedges Cup. There are also test matches against other countries.

The world's top tennis players come to Wimbledon every year for the Lawn Tennis Championships. They are held in the last week of June and the first week of July.

Horse races are held all year round. The famous races are the Derby, first held in 1780, and now run every year in June, and the Grand National, which is run in April.

Britain's round of the world motor-racing drivers' championships is the Shell Oil Grand Prix. It is usually held in July at either Brands Hatch or Silverstone motor racing tracks.

World championship motor cycle races are held at major race tracks. Speedway racing takes place most weeks. Check local papers for dates and places.

The main showjumping events are the Royal International Horse Show in July and the Horse of the Year Show in October. Both are at Wembley, London.

Food

Here are some specially British things to eat and drink. Some of them are the specialities of certain areas. Most started as local dishes, even though you can now find them nearly everywhere. Try to find out if there is a local food when you visit a new area.

Poorer people used to eat **Yorkshire Pudding** in order to fill themselves up before they ate their roast beef.

Fish and chips. Chipped potatoes (introduced from France) were first sold with fried fish in 1865.

Haggis is a Scottish dish made from a sheep's stomach stuffed with liver, suet and oat-meal.

Cream teas are a speciality of south-west England. They consist of scones, jam and clotted cream.

The custom of eating **pancakes** on Shrove Tuesday began as a way of using up eggs before Lent.

Many of Britain's **cheeses** have the name of the town or county where they were first made, such as Cheshire, Leicester, Sage Derby, Red Windsor. See how many you can find.

There are several **cakes and buns** which are named after the place where they were originally made, e.g., Dundee cake, Banbury cakes, Bath buns. Look out for some more.

The East India Company began shipping **tea** to England in 1669, and by 1750 it was the most popular drink. The British are the world's greatest tea-drinkers.

Beer and cider have been brewed and drunk in England since the 13th century. The south west is famed for its cider. Look out for local beer names on pubs.

Festivals and Shows

Shows and festivals are often advertised on posters and in newspapers. Tourist offices and libraries can usually tell you about special events happening in their areas. For some of the big events it is best to buy tickets in advance.

The **Edinburgh Festival** is one of the biggest arts festivals in the world. It takes place every year in August and September. There are plays, films, concerts and exhibitions, and a military tattoo performed at the castle.

The Queen's official birthday is celebrated every year at the **Trooping of the Colour.** This is on the second Saturday in June at Horse Guards Parade, London.

The **Royal National Eisteddfod** of Wales is a festival of Welsh music and poetry. It is held in August and takes place in a different Welsh town each year.

Dancing round a maypole on 1 May is an ancient custom. Look out for it in country villages.

Morris dancers often appear at local festivals. They wear special costumes with bells on their legs.

Travelling **fairs** visit most towns during the year. Some places, like Oxford, have a medieval fair in summer.

Circuses began in Britain in the 1770s. There are now 23 circus groups which travel round the country giving shows.

On 5 November, people light **bonfires and fireworks** in memory Guy Fawkes' attempt to blow up the Houses of Parliament in 1605.

On Christmas Eve, **carol singers** traditionally go round and sing outside people's houses.

50

At the **Farnborough Air Show,** held in July, you can see all kinds of aircraft. The Red Arrow R.A.F. squadron, which specializes in aerobatics, gives flying displays.

The **Royal Tournament** is a display of military skills, including competitions between groups of soldiers, held at Earls Court in London in July.

Car manufacturers from all over the world show off their latest cars every October at the **International Motor Show** at the Exhibition Centre, Birmingham.

County **agricultural shows** are held throughout Britain in the summer months. Farmers compete to win prizes for the best animals.

Sheep dog trials test how good dogs are at rounding up sheep. National trials are held every summer.

Dogs of all kinds can be seen at **Cruft's International Dog Show** held every February at Olympia, London.

The **Chelsea Flower Show** is world famous. It is held in the gardens of Chelsea Royal Hospital in London every May.

In Scotland, there are **Highland Gatherings** where you can see piping and dancing and athletic contests.

Rowing teams from all over the world compete in the famous **regatta** held on the Thames at Henley.

Veteran cars can be seen taking part in the R.A.C. London to Brighton Run in November.

London I

Great Britain's capital city, London, is the ninth largest city in the world and has over seven million people. The oldest part, now the business and banking centre, is called the City. You can still see the remains of a wall the Romans built round it. London's famous shops, theatres and hotels are next to the City, in the West End. Here are some suggestions of things to do and see in London.

Buckingham Palace. The London home of the Queen. If the flag is flying on top it means she is at home. You can visit the Royal Mews where her horses and carriages are kept.

The Houses of Parliament consist of the House of Commons and the House of Lords. Members meet here to discuss and pass laws. Big Ben is the bell inside the clock tower.

Westminster Abbey. Since 1066, all English kings and queens have been crowned here. You can see the tombs of most of them and of many other famous people buried here.

Trafalgar Square. Famous for its pigeons. On the column in the centre is a statue of Admiral Nelson, who defeated the French at the Battle of Trafalgar in 1805.

Piccadilly Circus is the meeting point of six main streets. In the middle is a famous statue of Eros (the Greek god of love) holding a bow and arrow.

The Tower of London. Built as a fortress it later became a prison and place of execution. The Crown Jewels and a collection of arms and armour are now on show here.

St Paul's Cathedral was built to replace old St Paul's, which was burnt down in the Great Fire in 1666. If you go there, visit the Whispering Gallery.

Parks

London is full of parks, gardens and green open spaces. Among them are ten big royal parks which were once the grounds of royal palaces. Many of them have boating ponds, lakes, playgrounds, statues and interesting birds and animals.

In **St James's** one of the royal parks, you can see pelicans and unusual ducks and geese which nest on an island in the lake.

This statue of Peter Pan stands near the Long Water in **Kensington Gardens** which join on to Hyde Park.

In **Richmond Park,** herds of fallow and red deer roam wild. If you are lucky you might also see a fox or weasel.

Regent's Park contains London Zoo. It is one of the biggest zoos in the world and has a collection of over 6,600 animals.

In **Crystal Palace Park,** there are life-size models of dinosaurs on islands in the boating lake.

Ceremonies and uniforms

The Changing of the Guard at Buckingham Palace. The new guard, led by a band, arrives to take over from the old guard. The ceremony lasts half an hour.*

The Changing of the Horse Guards at Horse Guards arch, Whitehall. This gateway is guarded because it was once an entrance to the grounds of the old palace of Whitehall.

Yeomen Warders (Beefeaters) guard the Tower of London. They sometimes wear blue uniforms.

Chelsea Pensioners— summer uniform. These old soldiers live in the Royal Hospital, Chelsea.

The King's Troop, Royal Horse Artillery. Can be seen firing salutes on state occasions in Hyde Park.

*For times, check with Information Centres (see page 56).

London 2
The River Thames

Hampton Court   Westminster Pier   Greenwich
Kew Gardens
Charing Cross Pier
H.M.S. Discovery
H.M.S. Belfast
Tower Bridge
St Katherine Dock

In the summer, you can take **boat tours** starting from Charing Cross or Westminster Piers.

London grew up along the Thames and you can see some interesting places on its banks.
This map marks the places mentioned below.

Tower Bridge was built in 1894. It opens to let big ships through, though very few come this far up the river now.

St Katherine Dock used to be a place where ships unloaded, but is now a yachting marina with a hotel, pubs and shops. There are lots of boats to see, including old Thames sailing barges and a lightship.

H.M.S. Discovery was the ship used on Scott's Antarctic expedition (1901–4). It is now a museum.

H.M.S. Belfast, the largest cruiser ever built for the Royal Navy, is now used as a Royal Navy Museum.

The Cutty Sark, on show at Greenwich Pier, is an old "clipper" ship which was used for carrying tea.

The Old Royal Observatory in Greenwich Park is where Greenwich Mean Time is measured from.

Kew Gardens have a vast collection of trees and plants. The glass palm house above, has exotic tropical plants.

Hampton Court Palace, built in 1515, is full of treasures and has lovely gardens, which include a maze.

Famous streets, shops and markets

Whitehall is where the main government offices are. The monument in the centre is called the Cenotaph.

Fleet Street is where many newspapers have their head offices. Look for their names on the buildings.

Oxford Street has many big department stores and is probably the busiest shopping street in London.

Harrods is one of the most famous shops in the world. They claim they will get anything you want to buy.

Fortnum and Mason has an exotic food hall, selling food from all over the world. It has a special clock outside.

Hamleys in Regent Street is a famous toy shop which sells every kind of toy and game you can imagine.

Portobello Road Market. On Saturdays the road is full of stalls selling antiques and all kinds of junk.

Petticoat Lane Market is open only on Sunday mornings. It sells mainly household goods.

Smithfield Market is the biggest meat market in the world. It is at its busiest in the very early morning.

Art galleries

There are good art galleries all over London. The National Portrait Gallery, which has pictures of many famous people, is specially interesting. This is King Charles I, who was executed in 1649.

Theatres

London is famous for its theatres and there are several which specialize in entertainments for children. These puppets are from the Little Angel Theatre which performs fairy tales and stories.

London 3

Viewpoints

A good way of getting to know a city is to go to a high point from which you can get a good view.

Primrose Hill. From here and from nearby Hampstead Heath, you can look south over London for a long way. Good places for flying kites.

Westminster Cathedral. Main Roman Catholic Church. Go to top of tower by lift for view of central London.

The Monument. Commemorates Fire of London in 1666. Climb up steps inside hollow column for view of City.

St Paul's Cathedral. Walk round the outside of the dome or go right up to the ball 112m above the ground.

Post Office Tower. Can be seen from most other high points. Now closed except for the revolving restaurant.

Getting around

This sign marks the entrance to the Underground (tube) stations. A quick and easy way to travel.

You can see more if you travel on the top deck of one of London's famous double-deckers.

If you want to take a tour, you can go in a special sightseeing bus with an open top.

A taxi is available for hire when its sign is lit up. Wave your arm to stop one.

Information services

Here are some telephone numbers you can ring for information about London.
222 1234 London Transport Travel Enquiries (information about tubes and buses)
246 8007 Children's London (events of special interest to children)
246 8041 Teletourist (main events of the day)
730 3488 London Tourist Board Information Bureau.
If you are telephoning from outside London dial **01** before these numbers.

Interesting museums

There are so many museums in London that it would take years to see them all. The British Museum and the Victoria and Albert are two of the largest and most famous. This page shows things from some other museums you might find interesting.

Museum of London. Illustrates the history of London. This is the Lord Mayor of London's state coach.

Imperial War Museum. Weapons, models, uniforms, photographs from all wars involving Britain, since 1914.

Horniman Museum. Arts and crafts and natural history. These are from the musical instruments section.

Bethnal Green Museum. A museum of childhood showing old-fashioned toys, dolls and doll's houses.

Pollock's Toy Museum specialises in model theatres, dolls, teddy bears and other toys. It also has a shop.

Natural History Museum. Dinosaur skeletons, fossils and stuffed animals, birds and reptiles.

Science Museum. Models and machines showing the history of science. This is a model of the Apollo 10 space capsule.

Geological Museum. Gold, diamonds, precious stones, rocks and fossils and "Story of the Earth" exhibition.

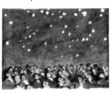

Planetarium. An expert gives a commentary while images of the night sky are projected onto the domed ceiling.

Madame Tussauds. Life-size wax figures of famous people, including a Chamber of Horrors.

London Dungeon. Very gruesome displays showing gory scenes from British history.

Useful Addresses and Information

The British Tourist Authority (B.T.A.) can supply you with addresses and telephone numbers of the various national and regional tourist boards, and also of tourist information centres in individual towns. The B.T.A. publishes a wide range of literature, some of which is listed below. Most titles can usually be obtained from a good bookseller.

British Tourist Authority, Thames Tower, Blacks Road, Hammersmith, London. tel: 01-864 9000.

Overseas B.T.A. offices

Australia: 171 Clarence Street, Sydney N.S.W. 2000. tel: 29-8627.
Canada: 94 Cumberland St, Suite 600, Toronto, M5R 3N3. tel: (416) 925-6326.
New Zealand: c/o Box 2402, Auckland.
South Africa: Seventh Floor, 107 Commissioner Street, P.O. Box 6256, Johannesburg 2000. tel: 296770.
U.S.A., 40 West 57th Street, New York, New York, 10019. tel: (212) 581 4700.

John Hancock Center (Suite 3220), 875 North Michigan Avenue, Chicago, Illinois 60611. tel: (312) 787 0490.

40 West 57th Street, New York, New York 10019. tel: (212) 581 4700.

Accommodation and travel

The following associations and publications will give you information about where to stay and how to get there.
Camping Club of Great Britain and Ireland Ltd, 11 Lower Grosvenor Place, London SW1W 0EY. tel: 01-828 1012/7.
Caravan Club, East Grinstead House, East Grinstead, West Sussex RH19 1UA. tel: East Grinstead 26944.
Ramblers' Association, 1/5 Wandsworth Road, London, SW8 2XX. tel: 01-582 6878/6826.

Hotels and Restaurants in Britain (AA).
Guide to Camping and Caravanning Sites, British and Continental (AA).
Recommended Hotels in Britain ed. D. Johansen, (D. Johansen).
Family Guide to England & Wales, Titchmarsh & Titchmarsh. (Jarrold Colour Publications).
National Express Coach Guide (for information on long distance coach travel around Britain).

Prehistoric and Roman

Here are the full addresses and telephone numbers of the places mentioned in the prehistoric and Roman sections of this book.
Butser Ancient Farm Demonstration Area, Queen Elizabeth Country Park, Gravel Hill, Horndean, near Portsmouth, Hants. tel: Horndean 595040.
Clayton Collection, Hadrian's Wall near Chollerford, Northumberland. tel: 043-481 379.
Housesteads Museum, Bardon Mill, Hexham, Northumberland. tel: Bardon Mill 363.
Lunt Roman Fort, Baginton, Coventry, West Midlands. tel: Coventry 25555, ext: 2662.
Richborough Castle, Richborough, Kent. tel: Sandwich 612013.
Roman Museum, Abbey Churchyard, Bath, Avon. tel: Bath 61111/65028.
The Roman Palace, Salthill Road, Fishbourne, West Sussex. tel: Chichester 785859.
Verulamium Museum, St Michael's, St Albans, Herts. tel: St Albans 59919.

Here are some useful books.
Discover Roman Britain (Shire Publications).
Discovering Archaeology in England and Wales by James Dyer (Shire Publications, which also publishes a series of regional archaeological guides).
Young Scientist Book of Archaeology by B. Cork & S. Reid (Usborne).

Castles and stately homes

Here are the full addresses and telephone numbers of the castles and stately homes mentioned in this book. Further information on these and other stately homes and castles can be found in the following book – *Visitor's Guide to Historic Houses, Castles & Gardens* (London & International Publishers).

Blenheim Palace, Woodstock, Oxon. tel: Woodstock 811325.

Deal Castle, Deal, Kent.

Hampton Court Palace, Hampton Court, East Molesey, Surrey. tel: 01-977 8441.

Harewood House, Leeds, West Yorks. tel: Harewood 886225.

Hatfield House, Hatfield, Herts. tel: (Curator) Hatfield 62823/65159.

Knebworth House, Knebworth, Herts. tel: Stevenage 812661.

Longleat House, Warminster, Wilts. tel: Maiden Bradley, 551. Safari park, tel: Maiden Bradley 328.

Oxburgh Hall, Swaffham, Norfolk. tel: Gooderstone 258.

Rochester Castle, Rochester, Kent. tel: Medway 402276.

Royal Pavilion, Old Steine, Brighton, East Sussex. tel: Brighton 603005.

Windsor Castle, Windsor, Oxon. tel: Windsor 868286.

Countryside

You can get information on places of historic or architectural interest, or natural beauty from:

National Trust, 36 Queen Anne's Gate, London, SW1. tel: (01) 222 9251.

National Trust for Scotland, 5 Charlotte Square, Edinburgh EH2 4DU. tel: 031-226 5922.

National Trust for Ireland, Taylors Hall, Back Lane, Dublin 8. tel: Dublin 783940.

For information on watermills and windmills contact:
Society for the Protection Of Ancient Buildings, 37 Spital Square, London, E1 6DY. tel: (01)-377 1644.

For information on national and country parks, and forest parks contact:
Countryside Commission, John Dower House, Crescent Place, Cheltenham, Glos. GL50 3RA. tel: Cheltenham 521381.

Forestry Commission, 231 Corstophine Road, Edinburgh. tel: 031-334 0303.

For information on birds in the wild contact:
Royal Society for the Protection of Birds (R.S.P.B.); Young Ornithologists Club (Y.O.C.), The Lodge, Sandy, Beds. SG19 2DL. tel: Sandy 80551.

Wildlife and farm parks

Here are the full addresses and telephone numbers for the wildlife and farm parks mentioned in this book.

Easton Farm Park, Easton, near Wickham Market, Suffolk. tel: Wickham Market 746475.

Falconry Centre, Newent, Glos. tel: Newent 820286.

Highland Wildlife Park, Kincraig, Kingussie, Inverness-shire PH21 1NL. tel: Kincraig 270.

Norfolk Wildlife Park and Pheasant Trust, Great Witchingham, near Norwich, Norfolk. tel: Norwich 872274.

Otter Trust, Earsham, near Bungay, Suffolk. tel: Bungay 3470.

Wildfowl Trust, Slimbridge, Glos. tel: Cambridge (Glos.) 333.

Worldwide Butterflies, Compton House, Sherborne, Dorset. tel: Yeovil 74608.

For further information on wildlife parks and conservation areas contact:

British Naturalists Association, 48 Russell Way, Higham Ferrers, Northants. NN9 8EJ.

For information on farm trails and farm open days, contact: **The Association of Agriculture**, Victoria Chambers, 16/20 Strutton Ground, London, SW1. tel: (01)-222 6115.

Fun things to do

Here are the full addresses and telephone numbers of the various fun things to do mentioned in this book:

Bekonscott Model Village, Warwick Road, Beaconsfield, Bucks. tel: Beaconsfield 2919.

Caithness Glass Ltd, Harrowhill, Wick, Caithness. tel: Wick 2286.

Dartington Glass Ltd, Glassworks, Torrington, North Devon. tel: Torrington 22321.

Dr Who Exhibition, Longleat House, Warminster, Wilts. tel: Maiden Bradley 551.

Petrifying Well, Dropping Well Estate, The Lodge, High Bridge, Knaresborough, North Yorks. tel: Harrogate 862352.

Santa Claus Land, Aviemore Centre, Aviemore, Inverness-shire. tel: Aviemore 810296.

Thorpe Park, Staines Lane, Chertsey, Surrey KT16 8PN. tel: Chertsey 62633.

Below are some ways of finding out more information.
For festivals and shows, read: *Britain: Events* (B.T.A.).

For local workshops, contact: **Council for Small Industries in Rural Areas (COSIRA)**, 11 Cowley Street, London, SW1. tel: (01)-920 7134.

For sports information, contact: **Sports Council**, 70 Brompton Road, London SW3 1EX. tel: 01-589 3411.

To find out about steam trains, contact:
Association of Railway Preservation Societies, Sheringham Station, Norfolk. tel: Sheringham 822045.

For a list of zoos in Britain, look at: *Spotter's Guide to Zoo Animals* (Usborne).

Museums

Here are the full addresses and telephone numbers for all the museums mentioned in this book (other than those in London). Information about all the museums in Great Britain can be found in *Museums & Galleries in Great Britain & Ireland* (British Leisure Publications).

Industrial museums:
Gladstone Pottery Museum, Uttoxeter Road, Stoke-on-Trent, Staffs. tel: Stoke-on-Trent 319232/ 311378.

Ironbridge Gorge Museum, Telford, Salop. tel: Ironbridge 3522.

North of England Open Air Museum, Beamish Museum, Beamish Hall, Beamish, Stanley, Co. Durham. tel: Stanley 231811.

Weald & Downland Open Air Museum, Singleton, near Chichester, West Sussex. tel: Singleton 348.

Maritime museums:
Exeter Maritime Museum, The Quay, Exeter, Devon. tel: Exeter 58075.

Maritime Museum, Buckler's Hard, Beaulieu, Hants. tel: Buckler's Hard 203.

Royal Naval Museum, H.M. Naval Base, Portsmouth., Hants. tel: Portsmouth 733060.

Waterways Museum, Stoke Bruerne, near Towcester, Northants. tel: Northampton 862229.

Museums of special interest:
American Museum, Claverton Manor, near Bath, Avon. tel: Bath 60503.

Castle Museum, Tower Street, York, North Yorks. tel: York 53611.

Doll Museum, 'Fantasie', Nantygamar Road, Llandudno, Wales.

Museum of Childhood, 38-40 High Street, Edinburgh. tel: Edinburgh 225 2424.

Museum of Costume, Assembly Rooms, Bath, Avon. tel: Bath 61111.
Musical Museum, Kew Bridge, Brentford, Middlesex. tel: 01-560 8108.

Transport museums:
National Motor Museum, John Montague Building, Beaulieu, Hants. tel: Beaulieu 612345.
National Railway Museum, Leeman Road, York, North Yorks. tel: York 21261.
The Shuttleworth Collection, Old Warden Aerodrome, near Biggleswade, Beds. tel: Northill 288.
Tramway Museum, Matlock Road, Crich, near Matlock, Derbyshire. tel: Ambergate 2565.
London Transport Museum, Wellington Street, Covent Garden, London WC2. tel: 379 6344.

London

London Tourist Board, 26 Grosvenor Gardens, SW1 0DU. tel: 730 3488.
London Information Services telephone numbers are listed on page 56.

Here are some useful books and magazines:
A Capital Guide for Kids by Vanessa Miles (Allison & Busby).
Discovering London for Children by Margaret Pearson (Shire Publications).
Kids' London by Elizabeth Holt & Molly Perham (Piccolo).
Family London (London Transport).
Visitor's Guide to Central London (London Transport) This includes Underground and Bus maps.
Children's Guide to London by Christopher Pick (Cadogan Books).
This is your London (BTA). *What's on and where to go in London* (Where to Go Ltd) Weekly magazine.
Time Out Weekly.
City Limits Weekly.

Books and magazines

Look out for books in the following series:
Discovering (Shire Publications). Various counties and places to go, and other topics including caves, towns and watermills.
I-Spy with David Bellamy (Ravette Ltd). Animals and birds, the countryside and the seaside.
NatureTrail Books (Usborne). Wild flowers, wild animals, birdwatching and other natural history titles.
On Location (Bell & Hyman). Features of the environment, including rivers, roads and castles.
Pride of Britain Books (Pitkin). Guides to churches and cathedrals, famous cities and gardens.
Spotter's Guides (Usborne). Nature titles, including birds, trees, insects, shells, fishes and seashore.

Look out also for:
Museums & Galleries in Great Britain & Ireland (British Leisure Publications).
Visitor's Guide to Historic Houses, Castles and Museums (London & International Publishers).
Here are some books containing things to do when you are travelling:
I-Spy with David Bellamy on a Car Journey.
I-Spy with David Bellamy on a Train Journey.
Piccolo Book of Travelling Games by Deborah Manley & Peta Ree.
Puffin Book of Car Games by Douglas Barnard.
Travel Games by Tony Potter & Moira Butterfield (Usborne).

Index

AA, 28
abbeys, 18
aeroplane museum, 44
agricultural shows, 51
airports, 42
almshouses, 30
American museum, 45
amphitheatres, Roman, 9
ancient sites,
    prehistoric, 6, 7, 11
    Roman, 11
aquarium, 46
aqueduct, 37
arch, 41
architecture, styles of, 15, 22, 34
armour,
    Roman, 11
    suit of, 13
arrow slit, 14
art galleries, in London, 55

bailey, 12
baler, 39
banks,
    opening hours, 4
    signs, 27
barrows,
    prehistoric, 7, 11
    Roman, 11
Bath, 9, 24
baths, Roman, 8, 9
beam holes, 14
Beefeaters, 53
bells, church, 23
bishop's throne, 18
blacksmiths, 43
Blenheim Palace, 15
boats, 44
boat trips, 42, 54
boundary signs, 28
box-framed houses, 34
box pew, 20
brasses, 23
brass-rubbing, 23
bridges, types of, 37
brochs, 6
Bronze Age, 6, 7
Buckingham Palace, 52, 53
buses, in London, 55
butterflies, 47
buttresses, flying, 20

Cambridge, 24
camera obscura, 43
canals, 36, 44
Cardiff, 4
car museum, 44
cars, 29, 44, 51
cars from abroad, letters on, 29
castles,
    famous, 12
    fortifications, 14
    prehistoric, 7
    sham, 13
    things to spot at, 14
    types of, 12, 13
    villages around, 32
cathedrals, things to spot in, 18
caves, 41, 43
ceiling, painted, 16
Cenotaph, 55
Changing of the Guard at Buckingham Palace, 53
Changing of the Horse Guards, 53
chapels, types of, 19
chapter house, 18
cheese, 49
Chelsea Flower Show, 51
Chelsea Pensioners, 53
Chester, 24
childhood museum, 44, 57
chimney stack, twisted, 26
churches, 18–19
    age of, 22
    style of architecture, 22
    things to spot in, 20–21, 23
churchyard, 19, 30
circuses, 50
cities, largest, 4
Classical style of architecture, 15
cliffs, 41
cloisters, 18
coast, 41
coastguard station, 41
coats-of-arms, 17
cob, 34
combine harvester, 39
countryside, 36–37, 38–39

cricket, 48
crops, 39
crosses, 30
cruck-framed houses, 34
Cruft's International Dog Show, 51
crypt, 21
currency, 4

Deal Castle, 12
Decorated style of architecture, 22
doll museum, 44, 57
dolmen, 7
dolphinarium, 46
doors, church, 22
dormitory, 18
dovecot, 31
drink, 49
Dr Who Exhibition, 43
ducking stool, 31
dungeons, 13, 57

Early English style of architecture, 22
Edinburgh, 4, 24
Edinburgh Festival, 50
Eisteddfod, Royal National, 50
Elizabethan style of architecture, 15
Eros, statue of, 52

fairs, travelling, 50
falcons, 47
family crests, 17
fan vaulting, 20
farm,
    buildings, 38
    Iron Age, 7
    machinery, 39
    parks, 47
Farnborough Air Show, 51
fault, 41
festivals, 50–51
field crops, 39
fire insurance sign, 26
fire screen, 16
flag (Union Jack), 4
flint, 34
flints, 7
folds, 41
food, 49
football, 48
Forestry Commission, 37

fort,
  hill, 7
  Roman, 10
  shore, 10
four-poster bed, 16

gables, 35
gardens, things to
  spot in, 17
gargoyles, 20
Georgian style of
  architecture, 15
ghosts, 17
glass, Roman, 11
glassworks, 43
Gothic,
  castles, 13
  style of architecture,
    15, 22
Government, 4
great houses,
  famous, 15
  things to spot in, 16
Greenwich Mean
  Time, 4
gun-loop, 14

Hadrian's Wall, 10
haggis, 49
Hampton Court, 17, 54
harbour, 40
Harewood House, 15
Hatfield House, 15
hedge, 38
Henry VIII, 12, 17, 18
Highland Gatherings,
  51
hill figures, 7
horse races, 48
horse trough, 31
Houses of Parliament,
  52
houses, styles of, 34

Iron Age, 6, 7

Jacobean style of
  architecture, 15
jousting, 13

keeps, 12
Kew Gardens, 54
kite flying, in London,
  56
Knebworth House, 15
knot garden, 17

lectern, 21
lifeboats, 41
lighthouse, 41
  Roman, at Dover, 10
limestone, 34

link snuffer, 26
local museums, 26
locks, 36
lock-up, 31
London, 52–53, 54–55,
  56–57
  information services,
    56
  museums, 56
  population of, 4
Longleat House, 15, 46
lych-gate, 30

machicolations, 14
Madame Tussauds, 57
markets, in London, 55
Martello tower, 40
mason's mark, 26
maypole, 50
maze, 17
milecastle, Roman, 10
milestones, Roman, 9
miniature railways, 42
minstrels' gallery, 16
misericord, 20
model villages, 42
monastery, 18, 32
money, 4
Monument, The, 56
Morris dancers, 50
mosaic, Roman, 8
motor cycle races, 48
motor-racing, 48
Motor Show,
  International, 51
motte, 12
museums,
  aeroplane, 44
  American, 45
  car, 44
  costume, 45
  doll, 44, 57
  in London, 56
  Iron Age, 7
  local, 26
  maritime, 44, 54
  musical, 45, 56
  open-air, 45
  prehistoric, 11
  railway, 44
  Roman, 11
  toy, 45, 56
  tram, 44
  transport, 44
  waterways, 44
  weapons, 57
murder holes, 14
musical museums, 45,
  56

narrow boats, 36, 44
National Parks, 37
National Trust, 37
nature trails, 47
Nelson's Column, 52
Norman style of
  architecture, 22
nunnery, 18

oast house, 38
Old Royal
  Observatory, 54
open-air museums, 45
Ordnance Survey
  maps, 11
organs, church, 19
otters, 47
Oxburgh Hall, 15
Oxford, 24

panelling, linenfold, 16
parks,
  farm, 47
  Forest, 37
  in London, 53
Perpendicular style of
  architecture, 22
petrol station signs, 27
Piccadilly Circus, 52
pier, 40
pill-box, 40
pillory, 31
plough, 39
population, 4
portcullis, 14
porte-cochère, 25
portraits, 17
Post Office Tower, 56
potteries, 43, 45
pound, for stray
  animals, 31
prehistoric remains,
  6, 7, 11
pubs, 30, 49
  signs, 33
public holidays, 4
pulpit, 21
pump, water, 31
Punch and Judy, 40

Queen Elizabeth II,
  4, 12, 52

RAC, 28
radio masts, 36
railways,
  miniature, 42
  museum, 44
  steam, 42
refectory, 18
regatta, at Henley, 51

rivers, 36
River Thames, 54
roads,
    Roman, 9
    signs, 28
    types of, 28
Rochester Castle, 12
rocks, 41
Roman,
    numerals in dates, 23
    remains, 8–9, 10, 11
    sites, map of, 8
rood screen, 20
roofs, types of, 20, 34, 35
rose window, 20
Royal Pavilion, Brighton, 15
Royal Tournament, 51
rugby, 48

safari parks, 46
Santa Claus Land, 43
seaside, 40–41
seed drill, 39
sheep dog trials, 51
ships, 42, 43, 44, 54
shops,
    in London, 55
    signs, 25, 27
    types of, 27
showjumping, 48
shows, 50–51
shrine, Roman, 8
signs, 25, 27, 28, 33
Silbury Hill, 7
silent companions, 16
silo, 38
slate, 34
soccer, 48
spires, church, 22
spit, roasting, 16
sports, 48
squint, 20
stack, 41
stained glass, 23
stately homes,
    famous, 15
    things to spot in, 16
steam,
    railways, 42
    trains, 42, 45

stiles, 38
stocks, 31
Stone Age, 6, 7
Stonehenge, 6
St Paul's Cathedral, 52, 56
Stratford-upon-Avon, 24
streets, things to spot in, 25, 26
sundial, 17

taxi, in London, 56
television masts, 36
temples,
    mock, 17
    Roman, 8, 10
tennis, 48
tethering post, 31
thatch, 34, 35
theatres,
    in London, 55
    Roman, 9
tile-hung, 34
tolls, 28
tombs,
    in churches, 21
    prehistoric, 7
topiary, 17
torture instruments, 13
Tower Bridge, 54
Tower of London, 52, 53
towers, church, 22
towns,
    famous, 24
    Roman, 8, 9
    shops in, 27
    things to spot in, 25, 26
tractor, 39
Trafalgar Square, 52
trains, 42, 44
trams, 44
transport museum, 44
Trooping of the Colour, 50
Tube (Underground), 56
tumuli, 11

Underground (Tube), 56

uniforms, 53
United Kingdom, 4

vehicles, types of, 29
veteran car rally, 51
viaduct, 37
villages,
    prehistoric, 6
    types of, 32
    things to spot in, 30–31
villas, Roman, 8

wall anchors, 26
wall painting,
    Roman, 11
    church, 23
walls,
    farm, 38
    house, 34
    Roman, 9
    thatched, 35
wall-walks, 14
warming pan, 16
Warwick, 24
watermill, 36
water tower, 36
waterways museum, 44
weapons, 13, 14, 57
    Roman, 11
weather-boarded houses, 34
weathervane, 19
weepers, 21
Wells Cathedral, 23
wells,
    petrifying, 43
    water, 31
Westminster Abbey, 52
Westminster Cathedral, 56
whipping post, 31
Whispering Gallery, 52
wildlife parks, 47
windmill, 36, 43
windows,
    blocked up, 26
    church, 22
    rose, 20
Windsor Castle, 12

York, 24, 26, 44

zoos, 46, 53